## BASIC / NOT BORING LANGUAGE SKILLS

# READING COMPREHENSION

## Grades 6–8[+]

Inventive Exercises to Sharpen
Skills and Raise Achievement

Series Concept & Development
by Imogene Forte & Marjorie Frank
Exercises by Joy MacKenzie

Incentive Publications, Inc.
Nashville, Tennessee

Thank you to the students who contributed works
to this book. All written material, other than that in
public domain, is used by permission of the writers.

*About the cover:*
Bound resist, or tie dye, is the most ancient known
method of fabric surface design. The brilliance of the
basic tie dye design on this cover reflects the possibilities
that emerge from the mastery of basic skills.

*Illustrated by Kathleen Bullock*
*Cover art by Mary Patricia Deprez, dba Tye Dye Mary®*
*Cover design by Marta Drayton, Joe Shibley, and W. Paul Nance*
*Edited by Anna Quinn*

ISBN 0-86530-364-9

3   4   5   6   7   8   9   10        06      05

PRINTED IN THE UNITED STATES OF AMERICA
www.incentivepublications.com

# TABLE OF CONTENTS

# CELEBRATE BASIC READING COMPREHENSION SKILLS

Basic does not mean boring! There certainly is nothing dull about . . .

- . . . reading about skeletons in closets, slimy green stuff, or viewpoints of a headache
- . . . figuring out why you can't blow your nose in public in one U.S. town
- . . . seeing what you can find out from tombstones
- . . . deciding what ants and grasshoppers can teach you about life
- . . . untangling mixed-up words, sentences, stories, stereotypes, and ideas
- . . . learning how to cure acne or how to ride a 30-foot wave
- . . . tracking down clues for puzzles and mysteries
- . . . finding out humorous stuff you never knew about famous historical characters

The idea of celebrating the basics is just what it sounds like—enjoying and improving the basic skills of reading, understanding, and using words and language. The pages that follow are full of exercises for students that will help to review and strengthen specific, basic skills in the content area of language arts. This is not just another ordinary "fill-in-the-blanks" way to learn. The high-interest exercises will put students to work focusing on and applying the most important skills of reading comprehension while enjoying fun and challenging adventures with pieces of literature.

The pages in this book can be used in many ways:

- for individual students to sharpen or practice a skill
- with a small group needing to relearn or strengthen a skill
- as an instructional tool for teaching a skill to any size group
- by students working on their own
- by students working under the direction of a teacher or parent

Each page may be used to introduce a new skill, to reinforce a skill, or even to assess a student's performance of a skill.

As students take on the challenges of these adventures with words, they will grow in their mastery of language skills and will enjoy learning to the fullest. And as you watch them check off the basic reading comprehension skills they've strengthened, you can celebrate with them!

# SKILLS CHECKLIST FOR READING COMPREHENSION

| ✔ | SKILL | PAGE(S) |
|---|---|---|
| | Determine the meaning of words and phrases | 10 |
| | Identify literal main ideas | 11 |
| | Identify supporting details | 11, 14 |
| | Identify implied ideas | 12, 13, 27 |
| | Read to find answers to questions | 14 |
| | Identify elements of a story | 15 |
| | Explain sequence of events | 16–18 |
| | Identify cause-effect relationships | 19 |
| | Distinguish between facts and opinions | 20, 21 |
| | Summarize a written text | 22 |
| | Paraphrase a written text | 10 |
| | Choose the best title for a selection | 19 |
| | Make generalizations based on material read | 23 |
| | Draw logical conclusions from written material | 24, 25 |
| | Predict future actions or outcomes | 26 |
| | Make connections between fiction and real-life situations | 27 |
| | Compare and contrast written pieces | 28, 44 |
| | Evaluate ideas, conclusions, or opinions from a text | 29, 30 |
| | Make judgments about ideas or concepts in a text | 30, 31 |
| | Explain uses and meanings of words from a text | 10, 13, 32, 43, 47 |
| | Find information in written material | 32, 33 |
| | Make use of graphics to understand a text | 34, 35 |
| | Interpret charts and graphs | 36 |
| | Identify and interpret symbols | 37, 43 |
| | Identify the author's point of view | 11, 28, 38, 39 |
| | Identify bias in written materials | 40, 41 |
| | Identify stereotypes in written materials | 41, 42 |
| | Identify persuasion in written materials | 42 |
| | Identify the author's purpose | 43, 46 |
| | Identify the theme of a written piece | 22, 46 |
| | Identify the tone of a written piece | 28, 44, 46, 47 |
| | Identify techniques that develop characters | 45 |
| | Identify many literary devices (such as similes, metaphors, personification) | 37–49 |
| | Identify figurative language | 37–40, 48 |
| | Explain techniques used by a writer to communicate a message | 37–49 |
| | Explain personal responses to written material | 50 |

# READING COMPREHENSION

## Skills Exercises

# RULES TO LIVE BY

It's great fun to play around with sophisticated words that are not normally used in everyday conversation. Below is a collection of phrases, written in "snooty" language, but offering some good, sound advice. Match each sophisticated phrase with its contemporary, vernacular translation. (If you don't know what *vernacular* means, look it up. By the time you get through with this page, it should be a word you will never forget!)

Write the number of each "snooty" phrase next to its matching translation in ordinary language.

1. Sustain thyself by engorging a goodly portion of the nutritious elements.
2. When the gray aurora dawns in the eastern hemisphere, rouse yourself to a vertical position.
3. Render to each homo sapien his rightful appurtenances.
4. Avoid premature surrender to excessive anticipation.
5. Please refrain from making your bowler a depository for sputum.

6. Ambulate with extreme vigilance.
7. Avoid contumelious comportment.
8. Never extricate foreign matter from your proboscis.
9. Shield your oral aperture when forcibly expelling from the same.
10. Regard with deference and esteem those who are your predecessors.

| | | | | |
|---|---|---|---|---|
| 9 | A. Cover your mouth when you cough. | | 5 | F. Don't spit in your hat. |
| 1 | B. Eat to live. | | 2 | G. Get up in the morning. |
| 4 | C. Be patient. | | 10 | H. Respect your elders. |
| 7 | D. Don't be rude. | | 3 | I. Give everyone his own stuff. |
| 6 | E. Watch your step. | | 8 | J. Don't pick your nose. |

Name _____

# GET AHEAD!

People do not like headaches. But have you ever wondered how headaches feel about people? An eighth grader wrote this clever essay that will give you some clues.

*Advantages of Being a Headache*

Fortunately, a headache never has difficulty finding a good home. A toothache has to hope for a vacancy in a holey molar. An earache must wait for a cold day to chase down hatless children, but I just move into a head any time.

Even if an earache is lucky enough to catch an ear, he has the most cramped quarters in which to live. And imagine how confining it is to be a toothache, trapped inside a bicuspid! Neither has as much room as I, and I don't have to tolerate either bad breath or sticky, yellow wax!

A headache can easily find lodging in any head that has a problem (and most people have plenty of problems!). Why, I've lived in some of the best heads—presidents, movie stars, and even athletes—I have known many of them intimately. I've met more people than any other ache around. Most of them I like, but the person I wish never to meet is the one who invented aspirin!

1. From what point of view is the essay written? *a headache's point of view*
2. What is the main idea conveyed by this essay?
   *What it's like to be a headache*
3. List at least three details that support the main idea you have written above.
   *headaches can always find a good home*
   *headaches get to meet many different people*
   *headaches don't have cramped quarters*

4. What does the writer say is the one disadvantage of being a headache?
   *aspirin*

5. Which title below do you think best fits this piece? Write it on the line above the essay.
   • Go to the Head of the Class
   • Down with Aspirin!
   • Advantages of Being a Headache
   • Heads I Have Met

6. Explain your title choice.
   *I chose Advantages of Being a Headache because that's mainly what the story is about. It talks about how earaches and toothaches are cramped but headaches aren't, and a few other things that make headaches better than earaches and toothaches.*

Name _____

# WANTED: TOP-QUALITY PERSON

In this famous poem, Rudyard Kipling describes what it takes to be a "real" or high-quality man. It seems he was writing to his son or some other young man; however, the qualities he describes are not specific to any gender. Today, we could read this poem as addressed to anyone—male or female. Several qualities he mentions are:

A. self-confidence   C. self-control   E. perseverance
B. patience       D. long-suffering   F. humility

However, these words do not appear in the poem. Underline in the poem the phrase(s) that describe each of these qualities and mark those lines with the appropriate letter.

## "IF —"
### BY RUDYARD KIPLING

If you can keep your head when all about you
Are losing theirs and blaming it on you;
If you can trust yourself when all men doubt you
But make allowance for their doubting too;
If you can wait and not be tired by waiting,     5
Or, being lied about, don't deal in lies,
Or, being hated, don't give way to hating,
And yet don't look too good, nor talk too wise;

If you can dream—and not make dreams your master;
If you can think—and not make thoughts your aim;     10
If you can meet with triumph and disaster
And treat those two impostors just the same;
If you can bear to hear the truth you've spoken
Twisted by knaves to make a trap of fools,
Or watch the things you gave your life to broken,     15
And stoop and build 'em up with wornout tools;

If you can make one heap of all your winnings
And risk it on one turn of pitch-and-toss,
And lose, and start again at your beginnings
And never breathe a word about your loss;     20
If you can force your heart and nerve and sinew
To serve your turn long after they are gone,
And so hold on when there is nothing in you
Except the Will which says to them: "Hold on."
If you can talk with crowds and keep your virtue,     25
Or walk with kings—nor lose the common touch;
If neither foes nor loving friends can hurt you;
If all men count with you, but none too much;
If you can fill the unforgiving minute
With sixty seconds' worth of distance run —     30
Yours is the Earth and everything that's in it,
And—which is more—you'll be a Man, my son.

Name

# A WORD TO THE WISE

"A stitch in time saves nine." "Fools rush in where angels fear to tread." "Look before you leap." These are some of the many proverbs or wise sayings we hear or read often. These quotes express ideas far deeper than the literal meaning of the words. For instance, the first saying below does not apply only to the task of gathering eggs from a hen's nest and putting them in a basket. What is its hidden or deeper meaning?

For each saying below, write your own explanation of its implied (hidden) meaning.

1. Don't put all your eggs in one basket. _____

2. Every cloud has a silver lining. _____

3. The nail that sticks up will be hammered down. _____

4. A bird in the hand is worth two in the bush. _____

5. Beware of wolves in sheeps' clothing. _____

6. The early bird gets the worm. _____

7. The squeaky wheel gets the oil. _____

8. Strike while the iron is hot. _____

9. Look before you leap. _____

10. A fool and his money are soon parted. _____

11. Fish and visitors smell in three days. _____

12. A rolling stone gathers no moss. _____

13. Keep your head in a crisis. _____

14. A stitch in time saves nine. _____

15. You made your bed—you lie in it. _____

16. Which two sayings are very similar in their meaning? #'s _____ & _____.

Name _____

# PUZZLEMENTS

Don't be fooled by the two simple paragraphs below. They are a lot trickier than they might look!
However, if you both read and think carefully, you should have no trouble straightening out the
puzzling questions.

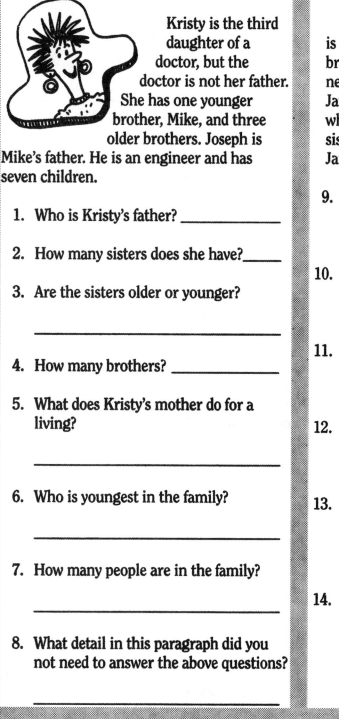

Kristy is the third daughter of a doctor, but the doctor is not her father. She has one younger brother, Mike, and three older brothers. Joseph is Mike's father. He is an engineer and has seven children.

1. Who is Kristy's father? _____

2. How many sisters does she have? _____

3. Are the sisters older or younger?

   _____

4. How many brothers? _____

5. What does Kristy's mother do for a living?

   _____

6. Who is youngest in the family?

   _____

7. How many people are in the family?

   _____

8. What detail in this paragraph did you not need to answer the above questions?

   _____

Peter's Uncle Dap is his mother's brother. He lives next door to Jamie's Aunt Tess who is her mother's sister. Jamie is Peter's sister. Marty is Jamie's brother.

9. Who is Peter's aunt?

   _____

10. Who is Jamie's uncle?

   _____

11. Does Dap have a brother?

   _____

12. Is Tess Dap's Aunt?

   _____

13. How many people in the story are related to Jamie?

   _____

14. What detail of the story is not helpful in sorting out relationships?

   _____

Name _____

14

# STORY BUILDING

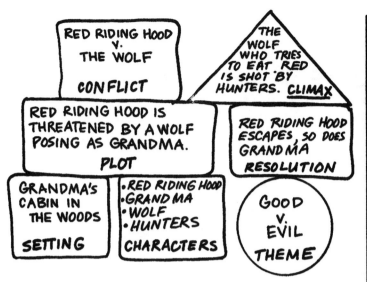

Elements of a Good Story

Setting - When and where the story takes place
Plot - Main events of the story
Conflict - A problem around which the story centers
Climax - The turning point (point of greatest intensity) of the story
Resolution - The ending—tells how the problem is solved
Theme - The main message of the story which illustrates a universal truth
Characterization - The way the players or the characters of the story develop through what they say, what they do, and what others say about them

It is easy to identify the parts or elements of a good story. They are the same, whether it is a nursery tale or a long novel. Sharpen your identification skills by reviewing the elements of the familiar "Little Red Riding Hood" story. Then use the second set of blocks to recreate the story of "The Three Bears" or any other story you have read.

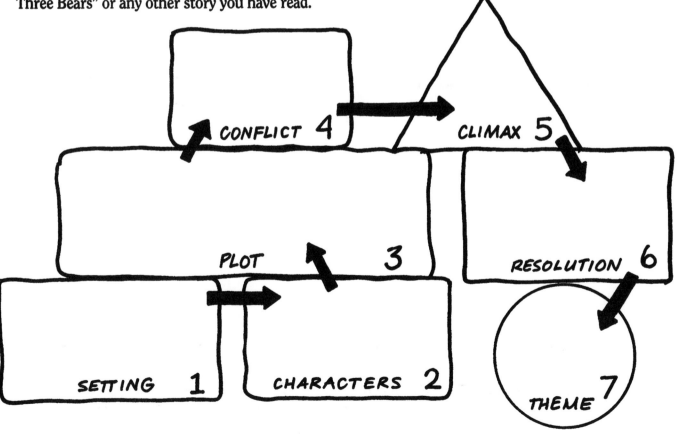

Name _____

# A FAMOUS LINEUP

A sprinkling of curious tidbits of information makes an otherwise boring collection of facts far more fascinating. Across the centuries, historians have written volumes about famous people. But only the cleverest of these writers have presented information in a way that is fun to read.

Read these excerpts from the works of a young, modern-day researcher. Then see if you can create a timeline that shows the order in which the famous subjects of this research lived and worked. Use the space provided on the next page (page 17).

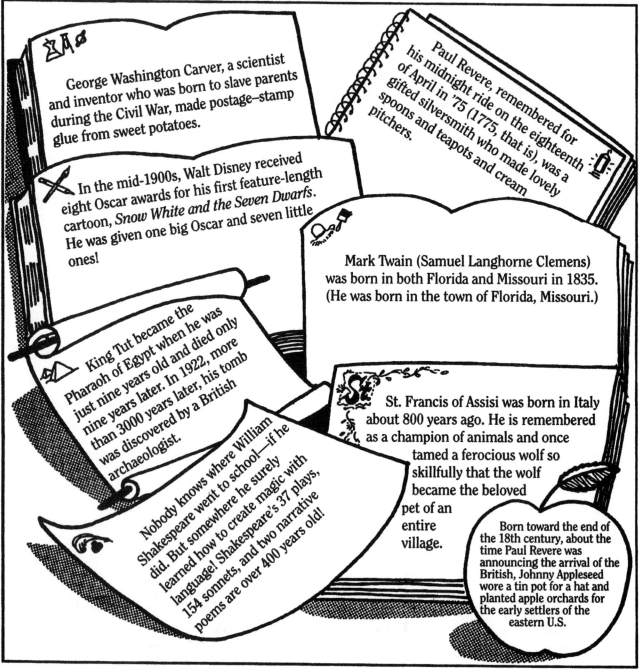

George Washington Carver, a scientist and inventor who was born to slave parents during the Civil War, made postage–stamp glue from sweet potatoes.

Paul Revere, remembered for his midnight ride on the eighteenth of April in '75 (1775, that is), was a gifted silversmith who made lovely spoons and teapots and cream pitchers.

In the mid-1900s, Walt Disney received eight Oscar awards for his first feature-length cartoon, *Snow White and the Seven Dwarfs*. He was given one big Oscar and seven little ones!

Mark Twain (Samuel Langhorne Clemens) was born in both Florida and Missouri in 1835. (He was born in the town of Florida, Missouri.)

King Tut became the Pharaoh of Egypt when he was just nine years old and died only nine years later. In 1922, more than 3000 years later, his tomb was discovered by a British archaeologist.

Nobody knows where William Shakespeare went to school—if he did. But somewhere he surely learned how to create magic with language! Shakespeare's 37 plays, 154 sonnets, and two narrative poems are over 400 years old!

St. Francis of Assisi was born in Italy about 800 years ago. He is remembered as a champion of animals and once tamed a ferocious wolf so skillfully that the wolf became the beloved pet of an entire village.

Born toward the end of the 18th century, about the time Paul Revere was announcing the arrival of the British, Johnny Appleseed wore a tin pot for a hat and planted apple orchards for the early settlers of the eastern U.S.

Use with page 17.

# A TIMELINE OF FAMOUS FOLK

Use with page 16.

Name

# BORROWED TROUBLE

LET ME TELL YOU, LET ME TELL YOU....

Have you ever had this experience? You meet a friend who is so excited that as she tells you what's happened she gets the events completely scrambled up. You couldn't possibly understand the story! Being able to relay events in the order they happen is an important skill. If you can't do it—no one is going to figure out what happened when.

Read the story below and follow the instructions to develop your storytelling skills.

---

As Albert rode home on the school bus, he thought about the wonderful time he'd had at the class picnic. There had been lots of food and games, but he'd enjoyed the softball game most of all. Since he'd borrowed his older brother's ball and brought it for everyone to use, the kids let him be a team captain, and his team had won. Later his friend, Ralph, asked Albert if he could borrow the ball and bring it back to him at school the next day. Albert had agreed and was feeling extra good that he had made Ralph happy.

When the bus stopped, Albert stepped off whistling. As he walked toward his house, he saw his brother and three friends sitting on the front porch. All the boys had bats and gloves and looked as if they were waiting for something. Suddenly Albert felt sick. He realized that they were waiting for him to bring back the borrowed ball . . .

---

Write the order of events, so far, in the unfinished story. When you have made a list of them, add to the sequence to show how you would finish the story.

1. _____

2. _____

3. _____

4. _____

5. _____

6. _____

7. _____

8. _____

9. _____

10. _____

Name _____

# FLIP-FLOP

Jason mistakenly ate a grub worm which inhabited a large tomato he had cut up for his salad. He got sick!

Jason became ill when he discovered one half of a grub worm in his salad.

Cause and effect in relationships can happen in either of two ways. The cause may be stated, followed by the effect, or they may flip-flop, as in the example above, and the effect may precede the cause.

Before each pair of sentences below, write **C-E** if the order of the sentences is cause-effect, and **E-C** if the order is reversed.

_____ 1. Jessica's parents sold her drum set. It was responsible for more noise than they (and the neighbors) could bear.

_____ 2. Brandon left his towel on the beach. A helpful lifeguard took him to the lost and found.

_____ 3. Hundreds of hikers were stranded in an early season snowstorm. National Park rangers had to work many hours of overtime in rescue efforts.

_____ 4. Lisa got a poor grade because she didn't do her homework.

_____ 5. In spite of the howling storm, Tom was warm and cozy in his tent. A bear had snuggled up next to him.

_____ 6. The students snickered when Mike entered the room. Later, he discovered his clothes were not properly zipped.

_____ 7. Several mice had escaped from the science lab; thus the seventh graders were doing most of their studying sitting on tabletops.

_____ 8. The class gulped audibly when they saw Miss Benson's purple-streaked hair.

_____ 9. Rosa's bank account was empty after she bought her skateboard.

_____ 10. The principal started interrogating students after she found the flag in the locker room and the volleyball uniforms flying from the flagpole.

Name _____

# FACT FINDER

"He's the funniest guy in the school!" "Mara's the best player on the soccer team!"
These sound like statements of fact, but they are opinions. If you lined up all the guys in the
school, asked 100 people to vote for who was funniest, and all 100 voted for one boy, then would
the first statement become a fact? If you collected the statistics on every game the team had ever
played and showed that Mara's stats were better than everyone else's, would that make the second
statement a true fact? What about all the players who supported Mara, passed her the ball, defended
against the other team, and without whom she could never have scored any goals?

Telling the difference between statement of fact and opinion can be tricky. Read the following
"factual" report, written by a young visitor to the state of Hawaii. Underline or highlight any
sentence or part of a sentence that is opinion rather than fact.

---

Hawaii is the newest of the fifty United States and is the most beautiful state of all. It is
6,450 square miles in area and is the 47th largest state. It is actually made up of a chain of
islands, and is the only state in the union completely surrounded by water. No wonder it is
the favorite playground of mainland Americans! The many beaches and miles of warm surf,
moderate temperature, the long hours of sunshine, beautiful sunsets, and brilliantly
colored flowers that bloom year round have made this state into a tourist spot sought out
by people from all over the world.

Main products of Hawaii are pineapple, sugar cane, tropical fruits, coffee, macadamia
nuts and fish. Recreation and tourism are the main sources of income for many islanders.
The first settlers to Hawaii brought much of their Polynesian tradition to the islands. Their
dances (including the hula), religions, chants and customs contribute much to the beauty
and richness of island life. Over the years, new arrivals have come to seek their fortunes,
build homes, and raise families, so the culture has taken on additional facets and flavors.
For this reason, modern Hawaii is sometimes referred to as the "population melting pot of
the world," making it a fascinating place to live and a delightful place to vacation.

---

1. How many phrases contain
   opinion?

   _____

2. Think of a good title for this
   report:

   _____

   _____

   _____

3. Tell why each phrase in answer
   #1 is not a fact.

   a._____

   b._____

   c._____

   d._____

Name

_____

# U.F.O.

## (UNEARTHING FACT & OPINION)

How well can you differentiate between fact and opinion? Below is a mixed list of facts and opinions. Identify each statement with an **F** (if it's a fact) or an **O** (if it's an opinion).

Have someone time you to see how long it takes. Ready—set—go!

_____1.  Girls are braver than boys.

_____2.  Blue and yellow make green.

_____3.  A dog will attack you only if you act afraid.

_____4.  Bread can be made from water and flour.

_____5.  Frogs are amphibians.

_____6.  Colorado has beautiful mountains.

_____7.  Today, computer E-mail is the most efficient means of communication.

_____8.  Julius Caesar was a Roman citizen.

_____9.  My father is 40 years old.

_____10.  The nation's worst problem is crime.

_____11.  All Americans should be patriotic.

_____12.  If you eat your vegetables, you will be healthy.

_____13.  You will love my grandmother's cooking!

_____14.  Teenagers love to dance.

_____15.  The best skiing is in the Swiss Alps.

_____16.  There are twelve months in a year.

_____17.  Boys keep very messy bedrooms.

_____18.  Democracy is the best form of government.

_____19.  Ghost stories are scary.

_____20.  The United States is bigger than England.

_____21.  This lesson is easy.

TELL US EVERY
FACT YOU KNOW

Check your answers. Then ask a friend to do the activity. Who is faster at unearthing fact and opinion? Who is most accurate?

Name _____

# A BELLY LAUGH BALLAD

A ballad is a poem or rhyme that tells a short story and is meant to be sung. Many ballads are love stories or tragic stories of death and betrayal. A few are humorous. Here is a very funny English ballad, written on a universal theme. Some of the words have been paraphrased from Old English. You will be able to figure out the others!

## GET UP AND BAR THE DOOR

It fell about the Martinmas time,
And a gay time it was then,
When our goodwife got puddings to make,
She'd boiled them in the pan.

The wind so cold blew south and north.
And blew into the floor;
Quoth our goodman to our goodwife
"Get up and bar the door."

"My hand is in my housework,
Goodman, you may see
And it will not be barred for a hundred years
If it has to be barred by me!"

So they made a pact between them two,
They made it firm and sure.
That whoever was the first to speak
Should rise and bar the door.

Then by there came two gentlemen,
At twelve o'clock at night,
They could neither see house nor hall
Nor coal nor candlelight.

They called, "Is this a rich man's house,
Or do you say it's poor?"
But ne'er a word would one of them speak
For barring of the door.

And first they ate the white puddings
And then they ate the black:
Tho the goodwife thought much to herself,
Yet ne'er a word she spake.

Then said one robber to another
"Here, man, take ye my knife;
Do ye take off the old man's beard
And I'll kiss the goodwife."

"But there's no water in the house,
And what shall we do then?"
"We'll use the pudding water
That boils in the pan!"

Up then started our goodman.
An angry man was he.
"Will ye kiss my wife before my eyes
And scald me with pudding bree?"

Then up and started our goodwife,
Did three skips on the floor;
"Goodman, you've spoken the foremost word;
Get up and bar the door!"

*I WILL NOT SPEAK A WORD! NOR SHALL I...*

1. What is the theme of this ballad?

   _____

2. What serious point or moral is made by this funny story?

   _____

3. Use the back of the page to write a brief summary of the story in this ballad.

Name _____

# LAWMAKERS GONE LOONY ?

In the state of North Carolina, it is illegal to sing out of tune! There was once a law in Boston, Massachusetts, that said that no one could take a bath in that city without a written prescription from the doctor. A Carmel, California, law prohibited women from taking a bath in a business office! Some of these laws are still on the books, although they may no longer be enforced. Pretty silly, aren't they?

People need laws to help them live together safely and harmoniously, but some laws are very peculiar. It boggles the mind to figure out what their purpose might have been.

Below is a list of laws that were actually enforced at one time in the United States. Read the laws. Think about why each law might have been written. Can you generalize what kinds of goals lawmakers had in mind when these laws were first enacted? At the bottom of the page, name three or four general purposes for making such laws. Then categorize each of the laws below by labeling them with the letter of one of the purposes you wrote.

## A LIST OF PECULIAR LAWS

_____ Walking with your shoelaces untied was against the law in Maine.

_____ If you were over the age of 88, it was illegal to ride a motorcycle in Idaho Falls, Idaho.

_____ In Phoenix, Arizona, all men were required to wear pants when they came to the town.

_____ In New Jersey, you were breaking the law if you delayed a pigeon.

_____ Trapping a mouse without a hunting license was against the law in California.

_____ In Maine, it was against the law to set fire to a mule.

_____ At one time, you would break the law in Louisiana if you whistled on Sunday.

_____ All beavers in Connecticut have the legal right to build a dam.

_____ In Minnesota, women's underwear and men's underwear could not be hung on the same clothesline together.

_____ It was against the law in Oxford, Ohio, for a woman to undress in front of a photograph of a man.

_____ Blowing your nose in public was against the law in Waterville, Maine.

_____ A dog has a legal right to bite, according to law in Colorado Springs, Colorado.

GENERAL PURPOSES FOR LAWS

A _____

B _____

C _____

D _____

Now, Now! Mixing "un-mention-ables" on the line is illegal in Minnesota, Mrs. Swensen.

Done at last!

Name _____

# TALES THAT TEACH

A hungry wolf could not find enough to eat. He saw a flock of sheep nearby, but they were so carefully tended by the shepherds that he could not safely steal in to grab his dinner. One night, he came upon a sheepskin that had been left by one of the shepherds. He placed it over his body and sneaked quietly into the pasture, taking his place amidst the crowded flock, unnoticed by the shepherds. And soon, he led a little lamb away to slaughter.

The next evening, he became braver and followed the shepherd back to the fold with the flock, dreaming of a tasty overnight feast. But the shepherd decided that he would have mutton for supper, and when he went with his knife to the fold, guess which was the first "lamb" he came upon! The lamb he killed turned out to be the wolf!

The logical conclusion or lesson that one may learn from this story is a deceiver often brings himself to destruction.

Carefully read the next story and see if you can draw the conclusion that the writer intended.

There was once a man who owned an amazing goose. Every morning, he visited the nest, and the goose had laid a golden egg. The man sold the eggs in the market and began to get rich. But soon, he became impatient; the goose laid only one egg a day and he wanted more money faster. Suddenly an idea came to him. He would cut open the goose and get all the eggs at once. But of course, when he cut the goose, he found not even one egg, and his wonderful goose lay dead!

1. What is the logical conclusion or lesson in this tale?

_____

Find the book *Aesop's Fables* and read these four tales: "The Lion & the Mouse," "The Boy Who Cried 'Wolf!'" "The Fox & The Grapes," and " The Ants & the Grasshopper." For each item below, write the name of the tale that reaches the conclusion or lesson shown.

2. Some people pretend to despise what they cannot obtain.

   Title:_____

3. Liars cannot expect to be believed, even when they tell the truth.

   Title:_____

4. You reap what you sow!

   Title:_____

5. A kindness is never wasted.

   Title:_____

DON'T MESS WITH ME!

Name_____

# THE DEAD TELL TALES

Tombstones often tell stories about the lives of the people who lie under them. Some of the epitaphs or inscriptions of long ago seem very peculiar by today's standards, but they give us some fascinating information about the people of those times. Read each inscription below and answer the question that follows.

A. Abel Silas McMahon, 1884, age 2 years
> In a moment he fled;
> He ran to the cistern and raised the lid—
> His father looked in, then did behold
> His child lay dead and cold.

How did little Abel die? _____

_____

B. Elisha Woodruff, 1816, age 70
> How shocking to the human mind
> The log did him to powder grind.
> God did command his soul away
> His summonings we must all obey.

What caused Mr. Woodruff's death? _____

_____

C. Seth Miller, 1848, age 46
> My wife from me departed
> And robbed me like a knave
> Which caused me broken hearted
> To descend into my grave.
> My children took an active part
> And to doom me did contrive,
> Which struck a dagger to my heart
> Which I could not survive.

What were the circumstances that lead to Seth's death?

_____

_____

D. Sally Dughy, 69 years old
> In the midst of society she lived alone.
> Beneath the mockery of cheerfulness, she hid deep woe.
> In the ruin of her intellect, the kindness of her heart survived.
> She perished in the snow on the night of Feb. 25, 1854.

What deductions can you make about Sally's life from her epitaph?

_____

_____

THE STORY OF BROTHERS

E. Joseph Hill, 1826, age 65
> My sledge and hammer be reclined
> My bellows too have lost their wind;
> My fir's extinguished, forge decay'd
> And in the dust my vise is laid.
> My iron's spent, my coals are gone,
> The last nail's drove, my work is done.

Can you guess Mr. Hill's profession? _____

_____

F. Caroline Newcomb, 1812, age 4 mos.
> She tasted Life's bitter cup
> Refused to drink the portion up
> But turned her little head aside
> Disgusted with the taste and died.

What is implied about the reason for this child's death?

_____

_____

G. This inscription was found on the tombs of two teenagers who died in 1814.
> How many roses perish in their bloom,
> How many suns alas go down at noon.

Write your own interpretation of those lines.

_____

_____

_____

Name _____

# THE END FROM THE BEGINNING

It's always fun to hear the beginning of a provocative story and then guess what the ending might be. "Hints" may be suggested or implied, but not revealed in the opening lines. Sometimes you have to "read between the lines" to find these hints.

Below are the beginnings of several very famous poems. Read these opening lines, then use the space provided below each partial poem to write what you think the outcome or ending of the poem might be—or could be. If you wish, you can research the real poem to find out how the original author ended it. (Your idea does not have to agree, but it would be interesting to compare the two outcomes.)

From "The Raven" by Edgar Allen Poe

*Once upon a midnight dreary, while I pondered, weak and weary,*
*Over many a quaint and curious volume of forgotten lore —*
*While I nodded, nearly napping, suddenly there came a tapping,*
*As of someone gently rapping, rapping at my chamber door.*

_____
_____
_____
_____

From a limerick in Edward Lear's *Book of Nonsense*, 1846

*There was a young lady whose nose*
*Continually prospers and grows;*
*When it grew out of sight,*
*She exclaimed in a fright,*

_____ !

From "The Highwayman" by Alfred Noyes

*The wind was a torrent of darkness among the gusty trees.*
*The moon was a ghostly galleon tossed upon cloudy seas.*
*The road was a ribbon of moonlight over the purple moor,*
*And the highwayman came riding—riding—riding —*
*The highwayman came riding, up to the old inn-door.*

_____
_____
_____
_____

Name _____

# LOOKING IN THE MIRROR

**Literature is like a mirror.** As we read, we often see ourselves or situations from our world. Through thousands of years of civilization, human beings don't seem to change very much. That's why stories that were written long ago still apply to us today.
**Below is one of Aesop's famous fables.**

> *One fine day in the late fall, a family of ants was busy drying and storing the bits of grain and seeds they had gathered during the long summer months when a very hungry grasshopper approached them and begged for a bite to eat.*
>
> *"What?" cried the ants, surprised. "Where is the store of food you have made for the winter? What have you been doing this whole long summer?"*
>
> *"I didn't have time to collect and store food," explained the grasshopper. "I was so busy making music, that before I realized it, the summer was gone by, and now I have nothing available to feed myself and my family."*
>
> *"So you were busy making music, were you?" replied the ants. "Very well, while we enjoy the winter feasting on what we have labored so hard to collect, you shall dance to your music!" And they turned their backs on the grasshopper and went on with their work.*

Use the space below to make a list of situations in which human beings behave very much like the ants and the grasshopper. Be able to explain your choices to a friend or your class-mates.

FEED THE GRASSHOPPER

A CRUMB FOR A TUNE ?

**Name** _____

# IT CAN HAPPEN...

Now and then, you read something that just seems to reach out and grab you by the heart—it stops you down and makes you think. Often your response is, "Yes, that's how I would feel if that happened to me . . ."

Two young writers created the pieces on this page. The first is by a third grader, the second, by a high school student. As you read them, take notice of the similarities and differences between the two works.

**I.**

There is a strange quiet in your house.

Your father is reading the newspaper, but not turning any pages.

Your mother is fixing dinner and slamming every cupboard door she opens. Nobody notices that you didn't hang up your coat. Nobody reminds you to practice the piano. That's how to tell there is an argument going on between your parents.

**II.**

*About every two years, my Aunt Ruth would go out and buy a new navy blue suit to be laid out in. She said it was important to look your best at your funeral. And every time we visited her house, all the cousins peeked in her closet and giggled at the lineup of unworn suits she had collected over the years. We laughed because Aunt Ruth was so young and sparkly—not the kind who was, at all, ready to up and die.*

*I remember how I grew up and got to be a teenager. But I don't remember how lively Aunt Ruth got to be this old, grey lady, lying so very still in a navy blue suit.*

1. Identify the tone of the two pieces (honest, anxious, morbid, friendly, distraught, realistic, sarcastic, frivolous, etc.).
   a. Tone of # I. _____
   b. Tone of # II. _____
2. Which piece would you characterize as most moving or poignant? _____
3. Which has more tension? _____
4. Which seems to have taken place over a longer period of time? _____
5. In which piece is the writer mainly an observer? _____
6. What is the point of view of # I? _____
7. What is the point of view of # II? _____
8. Which is NOT a true statement? Circle one.
   a. Both pieces are about the same subject.
   b. Both pieces are apparently a result of experience.
   c. Both pieces speak about a child's view of adults.
   d. Both pieces deal with an emotional event or crisis.

Name _____

# WE THE PEOPLE...

*On a certain day in November, millions of Americans stand in lines to vote for their preferred candidate. All evening long, they sit with bated breath and crossed fingers, watching a 13- or 19- or 22-inch screen as slowly, one by one, each state of the union turns a different color, showing which candidates won which votes.*

*Three months later, a young man—or maybe an old one—either ordinary looking or very handsome, Catholic or Protestant, liberal or conservative—steps up on a Capitol Hill platform and places his right hand on a Bible (should he be an atheist, it makes no difference), and swears to uphold the Constitution of the United States, which he, most likely, has never read.*

*Four years, he works long and hard, breaking most campaign promises he made. He fights with Congress and frequently disrupts prime-time television to deliver lengthy speeches on the American economy or to explain to the American people why it is their duty to help some other country who would rather we didn't.*

*America, land of the free, home of the hypocrite.*

Lindsey Williams, grade 12

1. Do you think that this piece is a fair representation of the election of a U.S. president? Why or why not? Explain your response.

   _____

   _____

2. Choose the word that best describes the tone of this piece: (Circle one.)
   objective      critical      cynical      supportive      light-hearted

3. What specific words or phrases in the writing contribute to this tone?

   _____

   _____

4. Is the article convincing? Why or why not?

   _____

   _____

5. Summarize the main message of the article in just one sentence.

   _____

   _____

6. Which statement can you best support?
   _____ a. The author is obviously ignorant about the U.S. democratic process.
   _____ b. The author sees the democratic process as lacking in integrity.
   _____ c. This article has no truth in it.
   _____ d. This article very accurately portrays the decline of democracy.

Name _____

    

# GOOD INTENTIONS OR INVENTIONS?

People often misuse words with which they are familiar, but don't quite "have a handle on." Unwittingly, they substitute a word they know, a word that has a very different meaning. See if you can catch the misused word in each quote and replace it with the word intended by each speaker. (Circle the word, and write the correction in the space at the end of each sentence.)

By the way, these misused words are called "malapropisms." This word originated from a character in Sheridan's *The Rivals* named Mrs. Malaprop whose misuse of words created a humorous effect.

1. Man paying his hotel bill: "I'm here to pay my accidentals." _____

2. Modern athletes have longer careers than athletes of the past because of Arabic exercises.

   _____

3. Speaker at an awards banquet: "I want to congratulate each of you for having extinguished

   yourselves." _____

4. This event is unparalyzed in the state's history. _____

5. We need to set a predicate of excellence in performance. _____

6. On a restaurant menu: "Dreaded veal cutlet with potatoes in cream." _____

7. School looking for volunteer teachers: Tudors needed! _____

8. Abe Lincoln signed the Emasculation Proclamation, which freed the slaves.

   _____

9. We were laughing historically at my mother's

   new hairdo. _____

10. Motorists need to stop for presbyterians

    walking across the street. _____

11. Governments ruled by kings and queens are

    called mockeries. _____

12. There was little water, so farmers had to irritate their crops. _____

Can you think of a few more malapropisms?

_____

_____

_____

Name

# OOPS!

Explain what's wrong about each of the following statements.

1. Four people were killed, one seriously, and eight more received slight injuries.

_____

2. One word sums up the responsibility of any vice-president, and that word is "to be prepared."

_____

3. A bachelor's life is no life for a single man.

_____

4. And now, the sequence of events, in no particular order.

_____

5. Today is an absolutely perfect day, and it's going to be even more perfect tomorrow.

_____

6. These are so valuable, you should buy hundreds and save them for your ancestors.

_____

7. It's permanent for now.

_____

8. He's overpaid, but he's worth it.

_____

9. Sign on a London street: No entry except for access.

_____

10. Space is almost infinite.

_____

11. Here is a plan for having some spontaneous fun.

_____

12. It's déjà vu all over again!

_____

Name _____

# CAMPUS NEWS

Vol. 90 Issue 13          September 27, 1996

# SPEAKING OUT ON HOMEWORK

**by Sara Frank**

An adult work day is eight hours. The work day for a high school student, especially a serious student, often exceeds that by two or more hours. Why should 14-to 17-year-olds have heavier workloads and work expectations than working adults?

How much homework should be given to high school students is a much debated issue these days. I would like to argue that high school students are given altogether too much homework. Students at Ashland High School say they average about 3 hours of homework per school night. That averages out to about 45 minutes per class. Often it is more than that—an hour or more for each class. In addition, they put in several hours each weekend on long-term assignments, book reports, and projects. Most kids also take part in after-school activities such as sports and clubs or jobs, which take up the afternoon and early evening. This doesn't leave many hours free before bedtime, and what time there is must be crammed full of homework. What this adds up to for many students like myself is that they start the day on the bus at 6:50 A.M. and arrive home at about 7:15 P.M. This means that after over 12 hours of school and school-related activities, they begin 2–3 hours of homework.

Teachers and many parents say that kids need a good amount of homework to help the learning process. They say kids need to practice what they learned in class that day. But shouldn't most of the practicing of new skills be done in the presence of the teacher? Since most high school classes meet 250 minutes or more a week (that's over 4 hours for each class), it seems that practice and at least a good part of individual homework could be done in class.

Doctors agree that teenagers need 8–10 hours of sleep a night to stay healthy. With such busy schedules, this amount of homework is hard to fit in with an adequate amount of sleep. High school kids today get worn out, tired, and sick because of the stressful, busy lives they lead. The many hours of homework each week really add to the stress. It robs kids of time to relax, socialize with friends, and do activities with families. It adds a lot of tension to their homes and lives. Teenagers need time to relax and have fun—which is what being a teenager is all about.

I don't believe that eliminating homework altogether is the solution. I am only arguing for a reasonable work load for teenagers. I recommend that teachers just should give less homework. They should teach as much as they can in class so kids can still learn, and have students do work in class where they can supervise and give them help. Teachers need to recognize that we are still kids and need to live a little. It might be good for them to think about whether it's healthy and helpful to learning to have teenagers working 12-hour days. Without the homework load, kids will be able to relieve some of the stress of being in high school. I believe that this, in turn, will actually help them learn better in school. They'll be more alert and healthy because they'll have a sane and enjoyable workday.

1. According to the author, how much time do teenagers spend on homework each week? _____
2. What main arguments does the writer use to substantiate her opinion? _____
3. If the writer has 3 hours of homework on a given night, how long would that make her "workday" (counting bus ride?)_____
4. What does the author list as the losses to a teenager due to the long school schedule?
   _____
5. Explain the meaning of the word "turn" as used near the end of the last paragraph.
   _____
   _____

Name _____

# IN NEED OF A CURE

Over the years, people have had all sorts of interesting remedies for various ailments—wrapping bacon around a sore throat, spreading cow manure on boils, curing a cough by drinking water in which you've soaked toenails—and such. Some are serious; some are rather humorous. Read these cures (written by kids) for common maladies, and answer the questions below.

If acne troubles you, one of these might work:
1. Wash your face every morning with prune juice.
2. Put toothpaste on each spot.
3. Rest 20 minutes a day with wet lettuce leaves lying across your forehead, nose, chin, and cheeks.
4. Rub strawberries or cucumber slices on your skin.
5. Wear a large hat.
6. Wear a high collar.
7. Grow your bangs very, very long.

**GUARANTEED CURE FOR ACNE TRY IT TODAY**

Find a good, healthy cow. Follow her around. (Not too closely.) Scoop up a small amount of cow manure. It won't take much, but it does need to be fresh. Mix this with cream cheese to make a smooth paste. Spread this on your face. Leave it on for 45 minutes each day, then wash it off. If it doesn't work, the cow will take back the manure.

Are you looking for a remedy for troublesome acne?
Alas, my friend, there is none.
Once you've tried them all, and given up—try this!
Glue a chocolate chip to each spot on your face, and nobody will notice the acne.

A BIG HAT HIDES A MULTITUDE OF FLAWS.

Acne troubled me for years; I couldn't find a cure.
I finally bought some paper bags; they did the trick for sure.
I cut some holes for eyes; I cut some for my ears.
I put one on each day for school; it served me well for years.

1. How many different cures are suggested for acne? _____
2. How many ideas are suggested that are not intended to cure the acne but to disguise or distract from it? _____
3. Which "cures" could be serious—and might actually work?_____
4. Which "cures" are probably intended only to amuse readers?_____
5. In the selection about chocolate chips, why do you think the author has used the word "Alas!"? _____

Name _____

# ADVANTAGE OR AD NAUSEUM?

The mailboxes of the western world are filled daily with all kinds of advertising and informational pieces. Some pieces attract readers; others disgust the receiver. Many offer a variety of choices and incentives to purchase, join, or subscribe. It's crucial to read ads carefully, so you know what you're getting for your money. Below is an ad designed to attract teenagers to join a teen health club. See if you can read and interpret it to answer the questions on the following page (page 35).

Use with page 35.

Name _____

34

Use with page 34.

# Join Now and Receive A
## free BONUS gift

YOUR CHOICE
T-SHIRT (S-M-L-XL)

WATER BOTTLE

**Join by March 1, 1998**

1. What tactics does the ad use to attract teenagers to join the fitness center? _____
   _____
   _____

2. What subscription comes automatically with all memberships? _____
   _____

3. What e-mail address can you use to get the center's hours? _____
   _____

4. What monthly fee must you pay to get the magazine subscription? _____
   _____

5. What membership benefits do you NOT get if you join at the $10 a month level? _____
   _____

6. If passes to the water park cost $15, how much do you save on water passes by joining at the
   $132 price? _____
   _____

7. What benefits would you get for $12 a month that you would not get for $9.00 a month? ____
   _____

8. Tickets to the DANCE CLUB parties cost $8 a couple. What do you save by getting these free
   with a $120 membership over what you'd spend on a $108 membership? _____

9. Which level of membership most interests you (and why)? _____
   _____

10. Do you think this ad will be effective in attracting teenagers to join the center? _____
    Explain your answer. _____
    _____
    _____

11. What do you need to do to get a free T-shirt or water bottle? _____
    _____

Name _____

# WHOLES & HOLES

It's Saturday morning. A group of middle-school friends who spent the night at Chad's house woke up to a breakfast of hot chocolate, donuts, and donut holes. Chad's mom could hardly believe the number of donuts and holes these guys consumed! See if you can find on the charts below the information needed to answer the questions that follow.

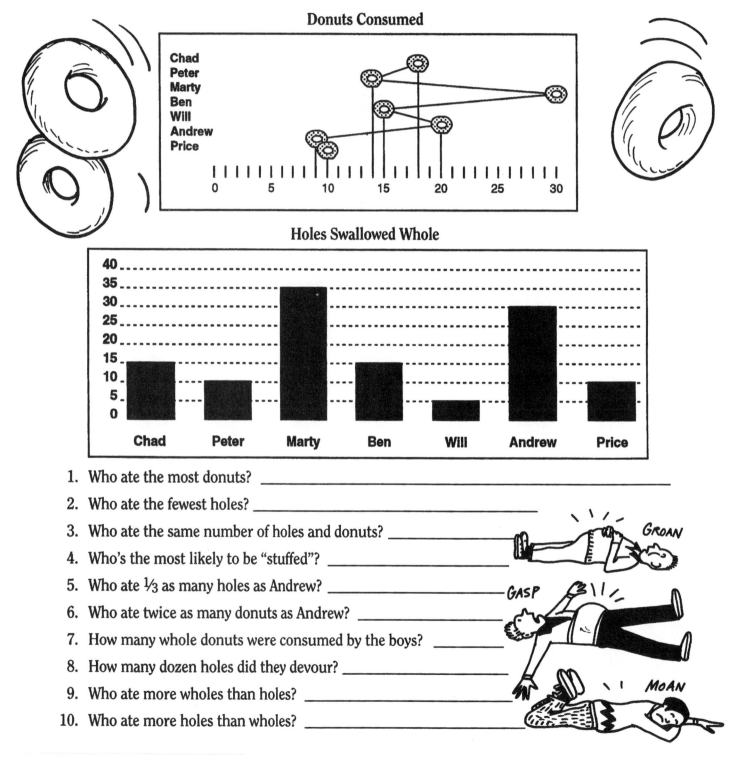

**Donuts Consumed**

**Holes Swallowed Whole**

1. Who ate the most donuts? _____

2. Who ate the fewest holes? _____

3. Who ate the same number of holes and donuts? _____

4. Who's the most likely to be "stuffed"? _____

5. Who ate ⅓ as many holes as Andrew? _____

6. Who ate twice as many donuts as Andrew? _____

7. How many whole donuts were consumed by the boys? _____

8. How many dozen holes did they devour? _____

9. Who ate more wholes than holes? _____

10. Who ate more holes than wholes? _____

Name _____

# FAIR OR FOUL?

Okay, so you can read words! Let's see how sharp you are at interpreting symbols to gain information about the weather.

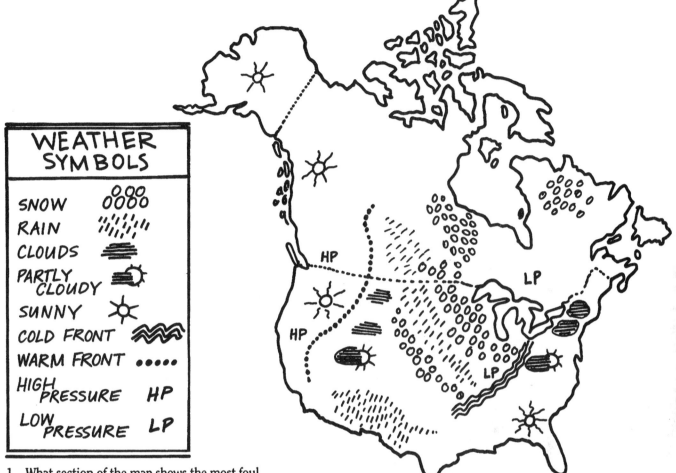

1. What section of the map shows the most foul weather?
   N.W. United States / S.E. Canada / N.E. United States / S.W. Alaska / Central United States

2. What section shows fair weather?
   S.W. United States / S.E. United States / N.E. Canada / N.E. United States

3. What type of front is crossing the U.S.–Canadian border?
   high / cold / warm / rainy / clear

4. Where is a high-pressure system located?
   N.W. United States / N.E. Canada / S.E. United States / Central U.S. / S.W. Canada

5. What kind of weather exists in the S.W. United States?
   snow / sunny / partly cloudy / rain / heat wave

6. When the cold front moves past the Great Lakes area, what do you predict will happen to the temperatures in the central southeast United States?

   _____

7. What sections of the United States have some spots that are partly cloudy?
   Northwest and South / Western mountains and Central East / Midwest and Southeast / Southwest and Northeast

8. Which of these sections are not showing precipitation?
   S.E. United States / Great Lakes, U.S. region / U.S. Central Plains / N.E. Canada

Name

# DOUBLE VIEW

The pieces below were written by high school students. Read both pieces carefully and then . . .

- On the line above each piece, create an appropriate title.
- Identify a single technique used by all three writers.
- Name other literary techniques used by individual authors.
- Decide from what point of view each piece is presented.
- Identify the experience being described by the author of each piece.

Record your responses in the spaces provided on page 39.

**I.** _____

*Temperatures rising at high noon,*
*Dry, parched, cracking lips*
*Yearn, burn and turn for*
*The drips of the succulent shimmer*
*Of the shimmy sham spam thing-a-ma-wham-bam*
*Liquid ice.*
*Trying to halt the frying,*
*Keep me from dying*
*While I am sighing, but not lying*
*About the stream that springs up . . . goosh, goosh, goosh*
*And cleanses my mouth*
*Like a spout*
*That makes me shout*
*To all about.*
*Energizing, Revitalizing,*
*Recognizing that what I need*
*For survival and revival equals*
*Two hydros plus one oxy!*

— Matt Lehman

**II.** _____

*Every time the phone rings, your heart skips a beat. You have begun to absent-mindedly write senseless poetry again. Your heart feels so full that you are afraid that it just might burst. Your body feels strange and incomplete. You seem to forget more than usual. You notice every red car that passes and hope it might be his. Your auditory senses have improved one hundred percent, except when you are talking to him—then you can't even understand your own words. This is how **you** know if you have developed a crush.*

— Kate Anderson

Use with page 39.

Name

# DOUBLE VIEW, CONTINUED

Use with page 38.

1. A single technique that is used by both authors is _____

   _____

   _____

2. Some other literary techniques, used by individual authors are:

   I. _____

   _____

   _____

   II. _____

   _____

   _____

3. From what point of view is each piece written?

   I. _____

   _____

   _____

   II. _____

   _____

   _____

4. Explain the experience being described in piece I.

   _____

   _____

5. Explain the experience being described in piece II.

   _____

   _____

Name _____

# ANONYMOUS PORTRAIT

Often an author will create a piece from his or her personal bias. In an effort to engage the readers, stereotypes may be used in the description of a character or a group of people to persuade the audience to share an opinion or merely to amuse them. See if you can identify the writer's attitude and purpose in this piece.

Sleepy-eyed, they enter the learning establishment at 7:43, meeting only the absolute minimum dress code requirements. In first period, they do their homework for second period, and in second period, they do their homework for third period . . . the vicious cycle goes on and on. Their bodies shift on a dime from being goofy and rambunctious to lethargic and sloth-like—being either uncontrollable hellions or stoic sleepers who couldn't care less if the world were ending in two minutes.

Yearning to be revolutionaries, they desire, at once, to be unforgettably awful, lovable, and admirable. This all-inclusive cult, holding the inferiors at bay, evolves into a tightly-knit squadron, struggling together toward tomorrow's aspirations, preserving its identity by body-slamming underclassmen against lockers and by exemplifying the carpe diem philosophy to its max. They are thrill-seekers, determined to suck the marrow out of life—a group of individuals, ascending the social ladder, overcoming numerous obstacles to become the few, the proud, the elite . . . .

— Matt Lehman, senior

1. What do you think is the writer's intended purpose? _____

_____

2. What is the tone of the piece? _____

3. Does the writer express a bias? If so, what is it? _____

_____

4. Identify and underline the specific words or phrases that create stereotypic images. _____

_____

5. About what group of people do you think the piece is written? _____

6. Give the piece a fitting title. _____

Name _____

# NOT YOUR USUAL GRANDMA

A mother wearing an apron, a little boy with mussed hair and dirty hands, a little girl with an angelic smile and a pink bow in her hair, a college professor with unkempt hair and glasses on his nose, a secretary filing her nails, a teenager on the phone—these are all stereotypes of people as we expect them to look and act in certain life roles. Of course, all mothers don't cook, all little boys are not covered in dirt, all little girls are not neat and bowed . . . but that doesn't stop the stereotypic image.

See if you can recognize stereotypes in the following items. Star all items that reveal a common stereotype. Then use the reverse side of the paper to write a description that dispels or is in striking contrast to each of those images.

1. The grandmother donned her glasses and nightcap and her wolf mask, pulled the quilt up under her chin, and called her grandchildren in to kiss her goodnight.

2. Tracy smoothed her blond ponytail and flashed a smile at the new senior quarterback. "Will I see ya' tonight?" she teased, as she bounced toward the cafeteria.

3. Grandmother appeared at the front door in her freshly starched apron, her white hair drawn tightly into a bun. "Children," she called. "It's time for milk and cookies!"

4. As soon as Dad finished cleaning up the kitchen, he was off to pick fresh raspberries for the tarts he had planned to make for supper.

5. The old man sat in quiet seclusion on his porch. Now and then, he would cock his head to catch the sound of a chirping bird or a chattering squirrel.

6. "Jumping Jehoshaphat!" exclaimed the old lady. "It's the first time I've ever gotten to ride behind a good lookin' man on a Harley!"

7. The CEO of a Fortune-500 company ran her delicate hand along the smooth edge of the impressive boardroom table. "Gentlemen!" Her young, vibrant voice was one of authority.

8. He swaggered into the bar, slid his denim-clad body onto the leather stool and hung the heel of his size 14 boot on the foot rail. "What's up, Jake? How's it goin' in Guitar City?" queried the bartender.

9. The preacher pounded the pulpit and railed against the evils of tobacco chewin', smokin', and drinkin'.

10. Sirens of the approaching ambulance whirred in the distance as the neighborhood bully knelt beside the still figure of a tiny girl, stroked her head softly, and fought back the tears.

Name

# A SYSTEM IN NEED OF REPAIR?

The passionate, thought-provoking essay you are about to read was written by a fifteen-year-old African American boy. Read it carefully to determine what message he is trying to convey to his readers. Write your answers to the questions below on the back of this sheet of paper.

*HAVE YOU APPREHENDED THE NOTORIOUS CAT BURGLAR, OFFICER?*

*A long time ago, you could walk down the street at night, in any American city, and you wouldn't have had to worry about your life being in danger. But in the last ten years, walking the street at night has become a game of Russian roulette.*

*The justice system has exercised almost every known power it has to stop crime and yet, the innocent often suffer while the guilty go free. In American it is not what crime you commit; it's how much wealth or power you have. Crime lords have broken practically every law; yet they are rarely brought to justice. The homeless, on the other hand, are constantly harassed by the police. When the upper classes demand the law, the cops respond in a flash, but when the poor and working classes need help, it takes the "overworked, underpaid" hours to come—if they show up at all. This is the harsh reality of the American system of justice.*

*YES, YOUR HONOR! I FOUND 27 HOT CATS IN HIS POSSESSION!*

*Our leaders believe that the only way to reduce crime is to install curfews, increase education, and convince citizens to get involved in their communities. But such ideas will only take care of the superficial troubles; the root problem still flourishes. For the danger doesn't hide on dark streets; it lurks in the dark hearts of men who are ignorant of or unwilling to acknowledge an absolute moral system of right and wrong. One study suggests that crime didn't begin its present upward swing until after prayer was removed from public schools. Of course, that is just one indicator; a connection between a morning prayer in a 6th grade classroom and a major change in the crime rate seems a far stretch, but is one of those small steps taken by a group of leaders that can become a big step for all mankind. After all, evil thrives when good men do nothing.*

- Dennis Upkins

1. What bias is evident in this essay?

2. Do you think the writer supports his bias with evidence?

3. Do you agree or disagree with his premise, stated in the first three sentences of the third paragraph? Why or why not?

4. What is the underlying message Upkins wishes to impress upon the reader?

5. In your opinion, is the essay persuasive? (Does the author convince you that most of what he says is true?)

6. Do you think your answers are influenced by your awareness of the writer's racial heritage? Why or why not?

7. Circle each word that demonstrates a bias or prejudice. Beside each circled word, write a plus (+) if you think the bias is favorable and a minus (–) if unfavorable.

| | | | | |
|---|---|---|---|---|
| heathen | obese | valueless | fashionable | beneficial |
| show-off | free thinker | across the tracks | comfortable | blue-collar |
| customary | independent | crackpot | nerd | guaranteed |
| elegant | old-fashioned | goody-two-shoes | out-of-date | upper class |

Name

# A POISON TREE

When an author wants to moralize or teach the reader a lesson, he or she often weaves the lesson into a story with the use of symbols that hopefully will grab the reader's interest and help to strengthen the lesson. William Blake, a famous English poet of the eighteenth century, uses a startling tale to warn his reader. Do you think his title is a good attention-grabber?

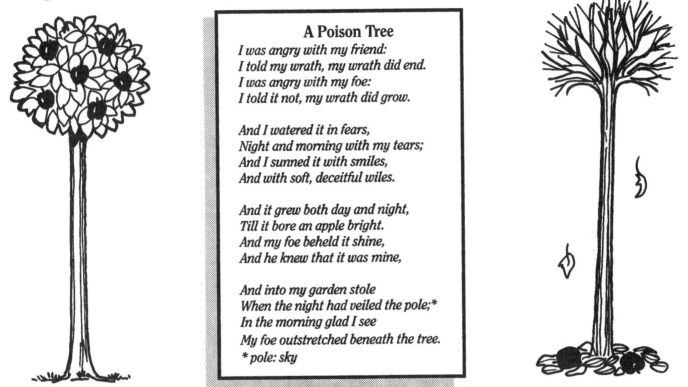

> **A Poison Tree**
>
> *I was angry with my friend:*
> *I told my wrath, my wrath did end.*
> *I was angry with my foe:*
> *I told it not, my wrath did grow.*
>
> *And I watered it in fears,*
> *Night and morning with my tears;*
> *And I sunned it with smiles,*
> *And with soft, deceitful wiles.*
>
> *And it grew both day and night,*
> *Till it bore an apple bright.*
> *And my foe beheld it shine,*
> *And he knew that it was mine,*
>
> *And into my garden stole*
> *When the night had veiled the pole;\**
> *In the morning glad I see*
> *My foe outstretched beneath the tree.*
> *\* pole: sky*

1. Determine the meanings of the words below and write them in the space provided.

   wrath _____  foe _____

   deceitful wiles _____  veiled _____

2. What occurred when the speaker expressed his anger? _____

3. What happened when he did not? _____

4. What "grows" out of the speaker's anger? _____

5. What symbol is used to represent this result of his anger? _____

6. In what other famous story is this same symbol used? _____

7. Why do you think the enemy comes into the garden? _____

8. What happens to the enemy in the garden? _____

9. Which statement best expresses the poet's message?

   a. It is wrong to get angry.

   b. Anger, kept to oneself, can fester and cause tragic results.

   c. Good friends always tell one another when they feel anger between them.

Name _____

*NO NEED TO USE THAT 'TONE' WITH ME, MARY!*

# WATCH THAT TONE!

The tone of a literary work is the writer's attitude toward the subject and toward his or her audience. A writer's tone may be friendly or hostile, intimate or distant and formal, serious or flippant, etc. Think how you might describe the tone of each work below. Beside each work that is familiar to you, write a word or phrase that describes the tone of that work.

*Adventures of Huckleberry Finn* _____

*A Separate Peace* _____

*Diary of Anne Frank* _____

*Les Miserables* _____

*Anne of Green Gables* _____

*My Antonia* _____

*Mary Poppins* _____

*Pocahontas* _____

*Cry the Beloved Country* _____

*To Kill a Mockingbird* _____

*The Wind in the Willows* _____

*The Borrowers* _____

*Little Women* _____

*Cheaper by the Dozen* _____

*The Black Stallion* _____

*The Red Pony* _____

*Alice in Wonderland* _____

*The Hobbit* _____

*THIS ALICE CHILD REALLY HAS AN 'ATTITUDE'!*

Choose one of the pairs of literary works or substitute any two familiar works you know that are similar in subject. Identify the tone in each piece and then write a paragraph in which you compare and contrast the tones of the two pieces. Use the back of this page.

Name _____

# MEET CHAUCER'S NUN

A writer may use a number of techniques to develop a character.
   1) By making a direct statement about him or her
   2) By showing character indirectly through action, thought, or dialogue
   3) Through observation and comment made by others in the story
   4) By using physical appearance and habits of the person to reveal his or her character

Geoffrey Chaucer, the second most famous British writer of all time (Shakespeare is the first) was a master of characterization. In *The Canterbury Tales*, he parades a variety of 29 characters past the eyes of his readers. Here's a paraphrase of one of his characterizations—that of the nun who traveled to Canterbury with a group of pilgrims.

In this piece Chaucer uses three of the techniques mentioned at the top of this page. Show which lines of the poem demonstrate each technique by writing the appropriate number after each line.

1.  There was also a Nun, a Prioress. _____

2.  Her smile was very simple and quite coy._____

3.  Her only oath by which she swore, "St. Loy!" _____

4.  And she was called by Madam Eglantyne . . . _____

5.  So dainty were her manners when she dined_____

6.  No morsel did she let fall through her lips, _____

7.  The sauce her fingers touched, just at the tips . . . _____

8.  So tender was she that she could not keep_____

9.  Composure at a trapped mouse, she would weep_____

10. If it were squealing, wounded, dead, or bleeding_____

11. Her little dogs she often was seen feeding _____

12. With roast, or milk, or pieces of white bread. _____

13. And deeply grieved was she if one were dead . . . _____

14. Softly on her face her veil did lay _____

15. Her nose was tiny and her eyes were gray;_____

16. Her dainty mouth was smallish, soft and red, _____

17. And smooth and fair, unweathered, her forehead . . . _____

18. A stylish cloak she wore with stately charm. _____

19. A coral trinket graced her comely arm. _____

I WEPT WHEN I SAW A LITTLE MOUSE BLEED TO DEATH IN A TRAP.

Name _____

# INVITATION TO THE GREAT OUTDOORS

IT'S SUCH FUN TO BE MOTHER NATURE !

*Can you keep a secret? Then follow me*
*Through meadows and woods to the open sea,*
*Through craggy cracks in city walks,*
*Through fields of scraggly, huskery stalks.*
*Run with me through Seasons' doors*
*And sneak through chinks in cabin floors,*
*Fly up and away to starlight skies,*
*Slide back on shadows just your size;*
*And then . . . then you'll begin to see*
*The secret . . . Shhhh. . .'tween you and me. . .*
*That the best, most beautiful, greatest stuff*
*Of which there's NEVER not enough,*
*Comes from Nature's lovely store;*
*Her shelves are filled with fun galore!*
*And except for things like paste or glue,*
*An occasional jar or worn-out shoe,*
*Perhaps some soap or snips of string,*
*You needn't have another thing —*
*'Cuz the lady who paints the day's sunrises*
*Has a zillion more surprises . . .*
*So leave your paper and pencil chores*
*And follow me to the great outdoors!*

1. What is the theme of this poem? _____

2. What is the author's purpose? _____

3. Which word best describes the tone of the poem?

       serious      playful      scolding      flippant      superstitious

4. If there is personification in the piece, write an example of it here: _____

5. If there is a simile in the poem, write an example of it here: _____

6. Write examples of other figurative language in the poem here: _____

7. Find at least three examples of alliteration: _____

8. Identify the rhyme scheme of the first 10 lines: _____

Name _____

# GREEN ISN'T SO BAD!

What comes to mind when you hear the word **green**? Do you think of negative or yukky stuff such as sickness or slime or jealousy? Or do positive ideas, smells, tastes, sights, and feelings such as spring, mint, youth, fresh veggies, or newness come to your mind? A group of kids pooled their individual lists of green ideas and wrote this collective poem.

1-*Green is the rhythmic chirping of crickets,*
2-*The way a pickle pinches your tongue,*
3-*And the dentist's fluoride treatments.*

4-*Green is mold and jealousy.*
5-*And the velvet stretch of a golf course.*
6-*Green is having the flu in math class.*

7-*Green stains the seat of your baseball pants,*
8-*Paints a forest of pine trees,*
9-*Drips slime on a slippery frog,*
10-*Dots a pond with algae,*
11-*Lends the music to a rushing stream.*

12-*Quiet is green*
13-*So is spinach, St. Patrick's Day, a lizard, and*
    *loneliness.*
14-*You are green when your heart is broken.*

15-*Green is sour.*
16-*Green is cold and crunchy*
17-*You can take green to the bank!*

IS THERE ANY OTHER COLOR?

NOT IN MY BOOK!

The poem is full of rich imagery and poetic devices. Identify the lines in which you find . . .

A. Personification: lines _____

B. Sensory images: lines _____

    (things you can taste, hear, smell, see, touch)

C. Emotion or feeling associated with green: lines _____

D. Alliteration: lines _____

E. How would you characterize the tone or mood of the poem? _____

F. What is the meaning of the last line? _____

Name _____

# THE SKELETON IN YOUR CLOSET

Do you know what it means to "have a skeleton in your closet?" Not literally—but figuratively? This young math student tells about the day a skeleton fell out of his closet.

*Everyone thinks I'm the big cheese in math class. But the real truth is that I have to beat my brains out on every assignment. Today the cat got out of the bag. Everyone saw right through me.*

*It was a lousy day anyway. I was down in the dumps the minute I woke up. Studying last night wasn't worth a hill of beans, and I knew I'd be in a pretty pickle when I got to math class. My brother was getting in my hair and driving me up a wall. Mom was fit to be tied when he and I got in a big fight. She almost bit our heads off.*

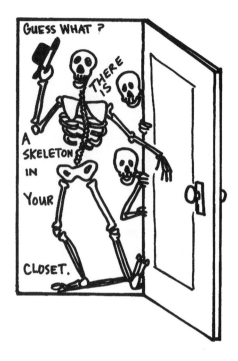

*On my way to school, it was raining cats and dogs, so my bike slipped on a corner and I bit the dust. At school, the math teacher was pretty burned up because none of us had finished our homework. I shook in my boots as he passed out the test because I knew I was in hot water. I was especially up a creek on the algebra problems. I blew the test.*

*I kept a stiff upper lip at school, but I sure needed to let off some steam. I held my tongue until I got into my room where I could throw things and scream my head off. One shoe went through the window—and now I'm really in the doghouse!*

This piece is loaded with figurative language. Underline or highlight each example of figurative language in the story. Count them. How many did you find?

Choose one of the paragraphs above and rewrite it in your own words. Try to use fresh, creative expressions instead of the phrases you marked above.

_____

_____

_____

_____

_____

_____

_____

Name _____

# PORTRAIT OF AMERICA

In the paragraphs below, two high school students (one a football player, the other an artist) draw very similar geographical pictures of the United States. Each creates a series of lovely images using figures of speech and sensory imagery. As you read, see if you can identify the primary literary device used by both writers.

## FROM SEA TO SHINING SEA

*In the tranquil forest of Vermont, stalwart, fragrant pines climb to the sky. Spanish moss covers ancient trees who spread their way from the Atlantic, across the Deep South, to where white sugar sands meet the transparent blue waters of the Gulf Coast. Rich golden grains, kissed with sunlight, stretch their arms across the Midwest toward winding, western rivers which twist through deep canyons, frantically searching for the perilous sea. Steep slopes, candy coated with a layer of snow, rest in the heart of Colorado before they make their last majestic rise toward the Pacific's blue and white, sun-crested waves. America— painting its way from sea to shining sea!*—Paul Armstrong

## THE HEARTLAND

*Early in the morning, the sun's golden rays peek over the symmetrical maze of crops; each section is a part of a giant, multi-colored quilt. A farmer peers out the farmhouse window and stares for miles at the beige, brown, maize and green patches of color along the flat country plain. Each square of the quilt blossoms with flavor and life; the majestic sun sprinkles a generous portion of beaming brightness onto every sleeping field. The rows of towering, crisp stalks of corn yawn as they stretch toward the sky, sipping their sunlight breakfast; strands of wheat sway gently in the breeze; little soybean plants squeeze their tiny finger-like roots into the soft, black earth. Every patch of the quilt tells its story with splashes of color, blazoned against the plowed soil. And when the sun goes down, the earth is warmed by the cozy quilt that tucks itself around the broad Midwestern landscape.*—Matt Lehman

1. What is the primary poetic device used by both authors? _____
2. Which author used an extended metaphor? _____
3. What comparison is made by the metaphor? _____
4. Underline each individual, figurative phrase in both pieces. _____

Can you guess which author is the football player? Probably not—though you have a 50-50 chance! Both write with tender sensitivity and joyous exuberance!

Name _____

# STOP THE CDS!

11777 Amazon Parkway
Deerfield, Illinois 60015

A.G.G. Music Company
1414 West Broadway
New York, New York 14415

August 15, 1996

To Whom It May Concern:

Please! Stop the CDs! They just keep coming!

I joined your CD program 6 months ago. I fulfilled my membership obligations a long time ago. I have paid all my bills. Furthermore, I have asked four times for you to cancel my membership.

But you just keep on sending me CDs and more CDs and bills and more bills. I'm sick of it. How can I get you to stop?

Do I have to get a lawyer?
Do I have to put a notice on the Internet about how lousy a company you are?
Do I have to dump old CDs on your lawn?
Do I have to write to the Better Business Bureau?
Do I have to call the president?

What will it take?

If there is a way to get you to stop sending CDs, sending bills, and sending nasty letters because I haven't paid the bills—PLEASE let me know.

Pretty Disgusted Cynthia

1. What do you think about the way Cynthia has chosen to communicate her opinions and feelings to the music company?

2. What do you like best or least about her letter?

3. How would you handle this same situation?

Name

# APPENDIX

## CONTENTS

# LITERARY DEVICES

**alliteration**—repeated consonant sounds in a phrase or sentence. These may occur at the beginning of words or within words. Alliteration sets a rhythm or mood to sentences and phrases. It is fun and pleasing to the ear and calls attention to certain words or phrases. (Example: *Peter Piper picked a peck of pickled peppers . . .*)

**characterization**—the techniques a writer uses to let the reader know about the characters. Characterization may let readers in on the traits of a character's appearance, personality, or behavior. These techniques may reveal the character's opinions, thoughts, or feelings, or these may let the reader see the reaction of other characters to that character.

**connotation**—all the ideas, feelings, experiences, traditions, or emotions associated with a word (as opposed to the literal dictionary definition). The connotation of *pirate* is black eye patches, swords, danger, high seas, deserted islands, fear, chases on the sea, buried treasure, parrots, black jackets, wooden legs, skull & cross bones, etc.

**denotation**—the dictionary definition of a word. (Denotation of pirate: *"One who robs at sea or plunders the land near the sea . . ."*)

**figurative language**—ways of using language that expand the literal meaning of words to give a new look at the topic. (Simile and metaphor are two common kinds of figurative language. Both compare a word to something else in order to embellish the look at the word.)

**foreshadowing**—a technique for plot development where an author gives clues that suggest developments or events that might come later in the story.

**hyperbole**—extreme exaggeration used to increase the effect of a statement or phrase. (Examples: *"This pie is to die for!" "He was so scared, he leapt a mile into the air!"*)

**imagery**—details that appeal to the senses. (Example: *"Sweet, slow drops of rich orange juice drip from the corners of my mouth and drool off my chin."*)

**inversion**—reversal of the order of words in a sentence in order to create a special effect. (Example: *"Dark the evening sky,"* instead of *"The evening sky was dark."*)

**irony**—a contrast between what appears to be and what really is.

**metaphor**—a comparison between two things that are ordinarily not alike. (Example: *"The toaster is a flaming dragon, breathing fire and blackening my toast."*)

**mood**—the feeling in a piece of writing. Mood is set by a combination of the words chosen, sounds used, setting, images, and details in a piece. Mood may give a feeling of beauty, honesty, silliness, darkness, fear, happiness, etc.

**onomatopoeia**—a use of a word that makes a sound which conveys its meaning—actually makes the sound of what it is or does. (Examples: *"Pop," "Slam,"* and *"Whoosh."*)

**personification**—the giving of human characteristics to a nonliving object. (Example: *"The river reached for me with icy fingers."*)

**plot**—a series of events that the author writes to construct the story. A plot usually involves the painting of a situation, a problem, or a conflict; the height of the conflict (or climax); and the resolution of the conflict.

**point of view**—the relationship through which or from which the story is told. A piece of literature may be presented from *first person point of view* (the narrator tells the situation, using "I"); *third person objective point of view* (the narrator is an outsider who describes the situation); *third person limited point of view* (the narrator is an outsider who tells what's going on in the mind of one character and speaks through that character) and *omniscient point of view* (the narrator knows everything and sees inside the minds of all characters).

**rhyme**—the repeating of sounds. Rhymes may occur within lines of writing ("the *clanging, banging* gong") or at the ends of the lines ("One, two, buckle my *shoe*. Three, four, shut the *door*.")

**rhythm**—the flow or movement of the sounds in words that brings a combination of stressed and unstressed syllables or sounds.

**satire**—a piece of writing in which the author makes fun of someone, a group, or a society.

**setting**—the time and place in which a story occurs.

**simile**—a comparison between two unlike things using the word *like* or *as* as a connecting word. (Example: "Our principal is *like* a vacuum cleaner because he's always digging up dirt.")

**stereotype**—a generalized belief or idea about a character, place, or situation. (Example: Swamps are stereotypically unpleasant, uninviting places; stepmothers are stereotypically evil; princesses are stereotypically pretty, sweet young women who stay in fancy castles rather than rebellious troublemakers wearing black leather and riding black horses or motorcycles around the countryside.)

**symbol**—a person, object, event, or place that has its own meaning but suggests one or more other meanings as well. (Examples: *An albatross is a symbol of a burden that someone has to carry or bear. A seagull is often a symbol of freedom. A dove is a symbol of peace.*)

**theme**—the main meaning or idea of a piece of writing. The theme includes not only the topic of the writing, but also a viewpoint or opinion about the topic.

**tone**—the approach or attitude that the writer takes toward the subject of the writing. Tone may be cynical, hostile, amusing, serious, frivolous, argumentative, playful, etc.

53

# READING COMPREHENSION SKILLS TEST

Each correct answer is worth 2 points.

Read these 5 poems and answer the questions below.

**B.**
The main thing about celery
is not the green
or the crunch
or the crisp
or the munch
The main thing about celery
is the thing
that stays with you
long after the celery is gone.
The main thing about celery
is
the strings.

**A.**
I'd sooner romance a gorilla
Or go to a dance with Godzilla
I'd sooner agree to be King Kong's mate
Than find stewed tomatoes on my plate.

**C.**
You need to have a stomach strong
To eat my mother's cooking.
Or else, bring a dog along
To feed it to when she's not looking.

**D.**
Don't expect me to eat oysters
because
The taste I could not stand
I'd rather swallow goldfish live
Or chew handfuls of sand.
I'd eat my walkman, eat the tapes
Chew my earphones any day
But put an oyster on my tongue
Are you kidding? No way!
You can torture me with scorpions,
Hang snakes from all my walls
Fill my bathtub with piranhas,
Push me over Niagara Falls.
You can swear to light my underwear,
Dunk me in boiling water to my hips.
No matter what you threaten—
Oysters will never touch these lips.

1. What is the common theme of all the poems?

2. Which poems have a humorous tone?

3. Write a phrase from the sausage poem which has strong imagery.

4. Which poems use internal rhyme (rhyme within a line instead of at the end)?

5. Which 2 poems contain the greatest number of descriptive words about their subjects?

6. Which poems make use of questions?

**E.**
Have you ever really looked at a sausage?
A slimy brown sausage, a hot blunt stinky sausage
With little pieces of grainy fat stuck in on the sides
A gushy fuzzy with mold reeking sausage
A wrinkly crinkly scabby sausage
Have you ever really looked at a sausage?

Name

A wall of water—it's the big wave that surfers wait for and thrill to ride. Millions of them all over the world rush into wild surf day after day—looking for that perfect big wave. Sometimes these perfect waves are as high as 30 feet!

And when they find it—how do they ride it? The idea is to ride along the vertical face of a big wave just ahead of the crest of the wave—the place where it is breaking. Of course, the surfer needs to stay ahead of that crest and not get crashed under it!

Surfers start by kneeling or lying on the surfboard and paddling out to the area beyond where the waves are breaking. Here they wait for the right wave. When a surfer sees a good wave coming, she turns and paddles furiously toward shore, trying to move as fast as the wave. If she times it right, the wave will pick up her surfboard and carry it along. At this point she stands up on the board at the top of the wave and rides it down the wall or vertical face of the wave. She actually gets going faster than the wave is moving. She must keep an eye on the wave's crest and turn the board so she stays ahead of it. If she gets it right the surfer can get a nice ride for several minutes—moving at a great speed—up to almost 10 miles an hour. Or, if she doesn't get it right, she can be be wiped out—sent smashing to the ocean bottom by the tremendous heavy weight and force of a monstrous wave!

7. What is the first movement of the surfer when she sees the right wave coming? _____

8. What part of the wave does the surfer ride? _____

9. At what point in the process does the surfer stand up? _____

10. What does the article tell about the size of surf-boards? _____

11. What will happen if the surfer doesn't stay ahead of the breaking crest? _____

12. Which is the best title for this piece? _____
    a. Why Surfing Is Dangerous
    b. Surfing Is Fun
    c. Riding the Wall
    d. The Structure of a Wave

# Off Her Rocker

Mother has lost all her marbles and flipped her lid! That's what we've decided. By 10 o'clock this morning she had blown her top 8 times. When the baby dumped his cereal on his head, she lost her cool. When Jenny put the cat in the washing machine, she got madder than a wet hen. And when Tommy ate her lipstick, she screamed bloody murder.

I think it was the toilet paper fort in the living room that was the last straw. She ran around yelling her head off about how we were pushing her over the edge and driving her up the wall. We tried to cool her down, but she sat outside for hours even though it was raining cats and dogs. When she came in, she wandered around in a fog the rest of the day. I tried to keep a lid on the little kids.

When dad got home, he was out in the cold about her bad day. So when he shouted, "Happy Birthday, dear, how does it feel to be over the hill?" he didn't understand why she went totally bananas and crowned him over the head with the frying pan.

THESE KIDS ARE DRIVING ME UP THE WALL!

13. How many figures of speech are used in this piece? _____

14. In paragraph 2, what does "keep a lid on" mean? _____

15. What figure of speech used in this piece means "didn't know anything"? _____

16. What is meant in the first sentence by "Mother has lost all her marbles"?_____

17. What is the meaning of "crowned" in the last sentence? _____

18. Which figure of speech means "getting old"? _____

Name _____

# TO TATTOO OR NOT TO TATTOO?

Tattoos have been around for hundreds of years. They've been found on Egyptian mummies, dating back to 2000 B.C. Ancient Greeks, Germans, Japanese, British, and people of many ancient tribes have used tattoos for various purposes. Often tattoos were (and still are) a mark of rank in society or a mark of membership in a particular group, tribe, or gang. Some tattoos were worn as protection against evil or ill fortune. Others showed courage. Tattoos were used to brand criminals, or to serve as disguises. But mostly, through history, tattoos have been used for decoration.

Today, tattoos are becoming popular as a fashion item of body decoration. The incidence of tattoos among many age groups is on the rise. Since the 1980s, women have been using the tattoo process for permanent eyeliner or lip color.

What, exactly is a tattoo? It is a permanent design decorating the human body. Tattoos are made by cutting or pricking the skin and inserting a colored dye or pigment under the skin. The modern tattoo process uses electric needles. In the past, instruments such as knives, thorns, and sharpened bones were used.

Is it a good idea to slice your skin and put color under it permanently? Many doctors don't think so. Serious side effects often accompany tattoos. Besides plaguing infections and eye damage from the permanent eyeliner, cancers have been linked to tattoos. Contaminated needles and equipment can also spread serious diseases, including AIDS. Many parents are irate that a child can get a tattoo without parental permission. A parent's signature is required in most states for ear piercing for a minor—yet kids can get tattoos without parental permission. One of the major concerns about tattooing is that there are no controls or restrictions on the process. No training or licensing is required for those who do it. As a customer seeking a tattoo, you cannot be sure of the person's ability, experience, carefulness—or of the safety or cleanliness of their equipment and supplies.

So think about this: when you get a tattoo—what else are you getting?

19. Which is *not* one of the reasons mentioned for tattoos?

    a) decoration  b) disguise  c) to frighten enemies  d) protection  e) membership in a group

20. What kind of tattoos are mentioned as relatively recent developments? _____

    _____

21. Tell two dangers of tattoos described in the article. _____

    _____

22. What is the meaning of "irate" as used in paragraph # 4? _____

23. In your own words, briefly explain how a tattoo is done. _____

    _____

24. What is the meaning of "contaminated" in paragraph #4? _____

Name _____

56

# CASE OF THE SABOTAGED LOCKERS

The mascot of the Northfield High School Rams, a small live ram, disappeared during the second half of the Homecoming Game. Frantic fans and school officials searched the football field, stands, concession booths, and locker rooms for hours—and found nothing. But on Monday morning, inside the school, some clues began to turn up. Five students whose lockers, numbered 116–120, were all in a row, reported that the locks were stuck and they couldn't get into their lockers. Furthermore, some strange sounds, smells, and liquids were emanating from the lockers. These were a curious mix of animal sounds and smells, food smells, and mysterious liquids dripping out. Authoritative school administrators and custodians flew into action, cracking open lockers and interrogating students—including the owners of the lockers: Matt, Michelle, Andrea, Scott, and Tara. This is what their investigations revealed:

- The custodians found one strange item in each locker.
- In locker # 119, custodians found a frightened, messy, squeaking rat.
- The ram was not in locker #117.
- Matt's locker is between Michelle's and Andrea's.
- Tara's locker has the lowest number.
- The locker next to Angela's held a large sausage-garlic pizza.
- Locker # 118 did not have any food in it.
- A bag of melting snowballs caused the liquid oozing from Scott's locker.
- The locker hiding the ram was next to a locker with 10 containers of Chinese food.
- Angela's locker is next to Tara's.
- The owner of the locker between the Chinese food and the rat is the culprit who kidnapped the ram and put all this other stuff in the lockers.

25. What is the only written fact found out about Matt? _____

26. Which locker numbers could not have held the ram? _____ and _____

27. Which event happened fourth of these five? _____
    a. Football fans searched for the mascot.
    b. The Homecoming Game halftime occurred.
    c. Students found their lockers broken.
    d. The ram disappeared.
    e. Pizza was found in a locker.

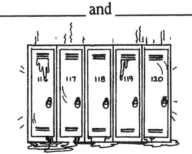

28. From the written facts, which locker could not have been Scott's? _____

29. What three roles did school officials take? _____

30. What is the meaning of the word "emanating" as used here? _____

31. How many places were searched before Monday? _____

Can you figure out:
    Which locker hid the ram? _____ Which locker-owner did the deed? _____

Name _____

Use these entries from the telephone book's yellow pages to answer the questions below.

**ANGELINO'S PIZZA**
Authentic New York Style Pizza,
Roasted Chicken, Calzone, Pasta
*Televised Sports—Free Delivery*
11 A.M.–1 A.M. 7 Days a Week
6666 Anton Parkway 668-9222

Chicago Style Deep-Dish Pizza
40 Varieties of Pizza
Take Out—Delivery—Dine In

692 Lakeside
862-0944

**B R U N O ' S   P I Z Z A**

## PIZZA DEN
We Deliver
Pizza • Pasta • Salad Bar
4 locations

| | |
|---|---|
| 16 E. Main | 772-1111 |
| 2770 Western | 774-1909 |
| 1402 N. 5th | 772-1414 |
| Northside Plaza | 772-6200 |

Voted Best Pizza in Town 1996

*Open 7 Days noon–midnight*

**PAPA G'S PIZZA CO**
Award-Winning Pizza You Bake at Home

**11 A.M.–11 P.M. Daily**

| | |
|---|---|
| Long's Plaza | 488-6111 |
| 20 N. Broadway | 488-0777 |

32. How many of these places deliver pizza? _____

33. How many of these places have more than one location? _____

34. How many describe the style of pizza they serve? _____

35. What does Angelino's have that no one else mentions (name 2 things)?

_____ and _____

36. What is distinctive about PAPA G'S? _____

37. Which establishment is open the longest hours? _____

38. Which two places have won some honor? _____

Name _____

# TEACHER'S FIELD TRIP BLUES

I am never taking this class on a field trip again! I mean it! Never! I have had it!

The trouble started, as it always does, with the bus ride to the aquarium. Jason somehow sneaked a bologna sandwich on the bus, even though I had collected all the lunches in my possession before we left school. We had been on the bus only 20 minutes when the sandwich ended up under Rosa Benson's bottom. The mustard was all over her white shorts, the bus seat, James's new jacket, and Jennifer's hair. I haven't figured out yet how it got in Jennifer's hair—she was 7 rows behind Rosa.

And this was just after Melanie sprayed hairspray on the bus driver and Louis threw up his breakfast.

I won't even try to describe the noise level on the bus, the damage to my ears, or the other bus disasters. I will say only that the chocolate milk in one fish tank, the wet clothes on 26 fourth-graders, the bad words yelled at the 2 nuns guiding a class from St. Mary's Kindergarten, the $20 bill Kim's mother was foolish enough to send along that is now in the belly of a shark, and the request from the aquarium guide that we refrain from visiting next year add up to more than I can take.

And while I'm complaining, I'll say that no helper I have ever taken along on a field trip is much help in controlling the chaos. Mrs. Vincent spent most of her time in the bathroom reapplying her makeup and hair after getting drenched in the dolphin show. And Mr. Hornsby said something like this every three minutes: "My children aren't allowed to be disrespectful." (His children were spraying drinking fountain water down the collars of primary students who were unfortunate enough to wander by) or . . . "Can't you do something to make these kids behave?"

"NO, I can't!" I said to myself, but not out loud. But what I can do is never, ever, set foot in a zoo, planetarium, airport, ice cream factory, museum, laboratory, or aquarium with anyone under 21—ever again.

39. Which of these events happened third?
    a. chocolate milk in the fish tank      c. Louis threw up
    b. mustard all over Rosa      d. Melanie sprayed hairspray

40. What is the meaning of *chaos* as used in paragraph #3? _____

41. What is the author's tone? _____

42. What is the piece's point of view? _____

43. Who sat 7 rows behind Rosa on the bus? _____

44. According to the written account, how many people got wet? _____

Match these literary devices with their descriptions

_____ 45. giving human attributes to a nonliving object    A hyperbole      G tone

_____ 46. an implied comparison without *like* or *as*    B imagery      H theme

_____ 47. extreme exaggeration    C personification

_____ 48. details that have concrete appeal to the senses    D irony

_____ 49. the main meaning of a written work    E metaphor

_____ 50. the attitude of the writer toward the subject    F simile

Total Score _____ (2 pts for each question)

Name _____

# SKILLS TEST ANSWER KEY

1. food
2. A, C, D
3. Answers will vary.
4. D, E
5. B, E
6. D, E
7. paddle toward shore
8. the face, just ahead of the crest
9. as the wave picks up the board
10. nothing
11. she'll "wipe out"
12. c
13. 19 counting title
14. keep calm
15. "out in the cold"
16. getting mad, or going crazy
17. hit, or smashed
18. "over the hill"
19. c
20. lip color, eyeliner
21. any two: cancer, infections, diseases, eye damage
22. angry
23. Possible answer: Slices or cuts are made in the skin, and color is put into the cuts under the skin.
24. unclean
25. His locker is between Michelle's and Andrea's.

26. #117 and #119
27. c
28. #116, because the article said the lowest number locker was Tara's
29. search for the ram; interrogate students; open lockers
30. leaking out of; coming out of
31. 4 (EXTRA: The ram is in locker # 118. Matt is the culprit.)
32. 3
33. 2
34. 2
35. Two of these: chicken, calzone, televised sports, NY style pizza
36. You bake the pizza at home.
37. Angelino's
38. Pizza Den and Papa G's
39. b
40. confusion, wild time, a mess
41. angry, disgusted, or cynical
42. first person
43. Jennifer
44. 27 (26 4th graders plus Mrs. Vincent)
45. C
46. E
47. A
48. B
49. H
50. G

# ANSWERS

## page 10

| | |
|---|---|
| A. 9 | F. 5 |
| B. 1 | G. 2 |
| C. 4 | H. 10 |
| D. 7 | I. 3 |
| E. 6 | J. 8 |

## page 11

1. the headache's; first person
2. head is the best place for an ache to reside
3. always a vacancy
   ears and teeth have less room
   ears have wax
   mouths have bad breath
   get to meet interesting people
4. aspirin
5. Answers will vary.
6. Answers will vary.

## page 12

Answers may vary slightly.
poem lines . . .
   1-2. C
   3-4. A
   5. B
   6-7. C
   8. F
   9-12. C
   13-16. D
   14-21. E
   22-23. F
   24-32. Answers will vary.

## page 13

1-15. Answers will vary.
16. 3 and 7

## page 14

| | |
|---|---|
| 1. Joseph | 10. Dap |
| 2. 2 | 11. no |
| 3. older | 12. no |
| 4. 4 | 13. 2 |
| 5. She is a doctor. | 14. Dap lives next door |
| 6. Mike | to Tess. |
| 7. 5 | |
| 8. Father is an | |
| engineer. | |
| 9. Tess | |

## page 15

Answers will vary.

## pages 16-17

| | |
|---|---|
| 1069 B.C.— | King Tut lives |
| A.D. 1200 — | St. Francis of Assisi tames wolf |
| 1564 — | Shakespeare is born |
| 1775 — | Paul Revere rides |
| 1800s — | Johnny Appleseed plants orchards |
| 1835 — | Mark Twain is born |
| 1860s — | George Washington Carver invents ingenious stuff |
| 1945 — | Disney wins Oscars |

## page 18

1. Albert borrows his brother's baseball.
2. He goes to picnic and plays games and eats food.
3. He loans the ball to his friend Ralph.
4. He rides the bus home.
5. He gets off the bus whistling.
6. He sees his brother and friends waiting; feels sick.
7. He realized his brother and friends are waiting for the ball.
8-10. Answers will vary.

## page 19

| | |
|---|---|
| 1. E-C | 6. E-C |
| 2. C-E | 7. C-E |
| 3. C-E | 8. E-C |
| 4. E-C | 9. E-C |
| 5. E-C | 10. E-C |

## page 20

1. 4
2. Titles will vary.
3. a. the most beautiful state of all
   b. favorite playground of mainland Americans
   c. fascinating place to live
   d. delightful place to vacation

Explanations will vary.

## page 21

| | | |
|---|---|---|
| 1. O | 8. F | 15. O |
| 2. F | 9. F | 16. F |
| 3. O | 10. O | 17. O |
| 4. F | 11. O | 18. O |
| 5. F | 12. O | 19. O |
| 6. O | 13. O | 20. F |
| 7. O | 14. O | 21. O |

## page 22

1. stubbornness or stubborn pride
2. stubborn pride can lead to trouble or foolish actions
3. Answers will vary.

**page 23**

Answers on both sections will vary.

**page 24**

1. One who is too greedy may lose everything.
2. "The Fox and the Grapes"
3. "The Boy Who Cried 'Wolf!'"
4. "The Ants and the Grasshopper"
5. "The Lion and the Mouse"

**page 25**

A. He fell in a cistern.
B. A logging accident
C. His wife and children left him.
D. She was homeless, insane, kind-hearted, and always seemed cheerful.
E. Blacksmith
F. She rejected life in this world.
G. Many die when they are only halfway through life—in their youth or prime.

**page 26**

Answers will vary.

**page 27**

Answers will vary.

**page 28**

1. Answers will vary somewhat.
   a. anxious
   b. friendly, honest, realistic
2. #2
3. #1
4. #2
5. #1
6. child's point of view; (third person limited point of view)
7. niece's point of view (first person point of view)
8. a

**page 29**

1. Answers will vary.
2. cynical
3. Answers will vary.
4. Answers will vary.
5. Answers will vary somewhat.
6. b

**page 30**

1. accidentals—incidentals
2. Arabic—aerobic
3. extinguished—distinguished
4. unparalyzed—unparalleled
5. predicate—precedent
6. dreaded—breaded
7. tudors—tutors
8. emasculation—emancipation
9. historically—hysterically

10. presbyterians—pedestrians
11. mockeries—monarchies
12. irritate—irrigate

**page 31**

1. Killed is serious—four were killed, not one.
2. "To be prepared" is three words, not one.
3. A bachelor IS a single man.
4. Sequence means to put in a particular order.
5. Perfect is an absolute—it can't be more perfect than perfect.
6. Your ancestors precede you in death—they're already dead.
7. Permanent is forever.
8. If he's worth it, then he can't be paid too much.
9. If you have access, you can enter.
10. Infinite is without end—it can't be almost without end.
11. If it is spontaneous, it can't be planned.
12. Déjà vu means to happen again, so the sentence repeats itself.

**page 32**

1. 15 hours plus several hours on weekends
2. Answers will vary somewhat:
   Kids have a longer workday than adults.
   The amount of homework is stressful.
   The long hours are not healthy.
   Kids should do most of the learning in class.
   Kids have little time for social and family life.
3. 15 hours and 25 minutes
4. social time, family time, relaxation, health, fun, sleep
5. in addition

**page 33**

Answers may vary somewhat
1. 10
2. 5
3. prune juice, toothpaste, strawberries, cucumbers, lettuce
4. cow manure, chocolate chips, and paper bags
5. to show discouragement or hopelessness

**pages 34-35**

1. attractive bonuses; good monthly rates
2. KEEPFIT
3. teenfit@atfc.com
4. $9
5. 4 passes to water park; 10 guest passes
6. $48
7. dance club membership; water park passes; guest passes
8. $180
9-10. Answers will vary.
11. Join by March 1, 1998

**page 36**

1. Marty
2. Will
3. Ben and Price
4. Marty
5. Peter and Price
6. Chad
7. 116
8. 10 dozen
9. Will, Peter, Chad
10. Marty, Andrew

**page 37**

1. Central United States
2. S.E. United States
3. warm
4. N.W. United States
5. rain
6. They will likely drop.
7. Western mountains and Central East
8. S.E. United States

**page 38**

Titles will vary.

**page 39**

1. a surprise element
2. I.  rhyme, metaphor, simile
   II.  sensory imagery
3. I.  thirsty person (first person)
   II.  person in love (second person)
4-5. Answers will vary.

**page 40**

1-6. Answers will vary.

**page 41**

Descriptions will vary.
The following items have common stereotypes: 2, 3, 5, 8, 9

**page 42**

1. bias against the present justice system
2-3. Answers will vary.
4. Crime cannot be eradicated by laws and systems alone. Every person of good will must get involved.
5-7. Answers will vary.

**page 43**

1. wrath—great anger
   foe—enemy
   deceitful wiles—underhanded acts
   veiled—hidden
2. anger disappeared
3. anger grew
4. fruit—evil results
5. apple
6. Garden of Eden
7. Answers will vary.
8. He dies, poisoned by the fruit.
9. b

**page 44**

Answers will vary.

**page 45**

Answers may vary somewhat.

Poetry lines . . .

| Line 1—1 | 11—2 |
|----------|------|
| 2—1 | 12—2 |
| 3—2 | 13—2 |
| 4—1 | 14—4 |
| 5—4 | 15—1 |
| 6—4 | 16—1 |
| 7—4 | 17—1 |
| 8—4 | 18—4 |
| 9—2 | 19—1 |
| 10—2 | |

**page 46**

1. How to escape to the great outdoors
2. To interest the reader in outdoor activity
3. playful
4. There are several examples:
   Seasons' doors, Nature's lovely store, lady who paints, her shelves are filled
5. none (Line 15 uses the word "like," but not for a simile.)
6. there are several: craggy cracks, scraggly huskery stalks, starlight skies, slide back on shadows
7. craggy cracks
   some soap or snips of string
   best, most beautiful
   filled with fun
8. aa, bb, cc, dd, aa

**page 47**

A. 2, 7, 8, 9, 10, 11
B. 1, 2, 3, 5, 8, 9, 10, 11, 12, 15, 16
C. 4, 12, 13, 14
D. 2, 8, 9, 13, 16
E. Answers will vary.
F. Money is green, too.

**page 48**

There are 23 instances of figurative language. Paragraph answers will vary.

**page 49**

1. personification
2. Matt
3. Gardens and fields are patches of a quilt.
4. Check students' individual pages.
   Paul is the football player.

**page 50**

Answers will vary.